A BALANCED HEART:

10 Weeks to Breakthrough

Katharine C. McCorkle, PhD

A Balanced Heart:
10 Weeks to Breakthrough
Copyright © 2011 by Katharine C. McCorkle

Balanced Heart™ Media
3145 Scenic Drive
Mars, PA 16046
724-776-5534

Cover Art by Robert J. Thompson
Layout and Design by Holly Rosborough
Editing by Gina Mazza

For information about custom editions, special sales, premium and corporate purchases, please contact Balanced Heart Media at 724-776-5534 or drkatie@balancedheart.org. Request for other permissions or further information should be addressed in writing to the publisher.

Library of Congress Control Number: 2011904451
ISBN: 978-0-9832182-3-4

This book is for informational purposes only, and is not intended to replace psychological or medical counseling, or other professional health care advice.

10 9 8 7 6 5 4 3 2 1

PRAISE FOR A BALANCED HEART

The heart as a symbol of love is perhaps the most universally known allegory. Science has now proven that "heart balancing" is the key to stress management. *A Balanced Heart's 10 Principles* help readers achieve maximum emotional health and wellness.

– C. Norman Shealy, MD, PhD,
Best-selling author of 90 Days to Stress-Free Living,
Founding President of the American Holistic Medical Association, and Holos Graduate Seminary

Dr. Katie has defined the spiritual process of emotional healing and given a step-by-step instruction manual for the journey. Her insights and simple way of presenting "the work" that all of us could be doing bring the possibility of our own emotional healing into probability. Dr. Katie has created a bridge between psychology and spirituality that will bring a sense of wholeness to anyone willing to take her instruction. Enjoy the ride and birth your dreams.

– Rev. RoxanneWilson, A Pathfinder Church

Energy follows thought, and *A Balanced Heart* provides scaffolding that allows us to make our dreams come true. The power of unconditional love catalyzes our insight as we are led through daily practice, resulting in a transformed life experience. This is an owner's manual for everyone who has a heart!

– Gregory J. Nicosia, PhD,DCEP, President of the
Association for Comprehensive Energy Psychology

Dr. Katie's no-holds-barred approach is, as she states, "simple but not easy." That said, if you follow the program, you really will accomplish that which you set out to do. Her "let's get it done" attitude allows readers to really move forward. If you want to accomplish your goals, this book certainly provides the means to do it.

– T. Love, Host of Energy Awareness Radio

Dr. Katie takes us on a spiritual journey with *A Balanced Heart*. In our fastpaced living, we often forget that our dreams are possible. These inspirational pages take the reader on a well-paced, intentional program. Each chapter causes you to slow down and take great pause, then listen to the way your spirit calls you to move. At the end you will have a clear understanding of your life's direction. Not only can you accomplish your dream, you'll be a better person for the effort. I highly recommend this book as a way to improve the mind and spirit.

– Linda May Conner, Director of Healthy Lifestyles,
Baierl Family YMCA

A Balanced Heart takes readers on a journey to explore a wealth of inner resources for seeking balance and wholeness in their lives. It illustrates practical tools for helping individuals reflect on their hopes and dreams, and developing strategies to pursue their dreams in an organized manner. *A Balanced Heart* takes a strengths-based approach, focusing on each person's assets and abilities and how to draw on them to grow and flourish. In a world in which it is often so easy to get caught up in extremes, *A Balanced Heart* provides a thought-provoking approach to seeking wholeness in one's life.

– Rick Chamiec-Case, PhD, MSW, MAR, Executive Director of
the North American Association of Christians in SocialWork

The doctor is certainly in, and so is her insight into what it takes to breakthrough. Providing a valuable timeline and day-to-day recipe for success, *A Balanced Heart* helps readers achieve inner peace like no other "how to" psychology book. Dr. Katie's 10 Principles are clearly at the core of this "breakthrough manual," as she spells out in great detail what transitions the mind, spirit and heart may encounter as they prepare for and deliver life-altering results. If you've got a dream but don't know where to start the dream-to-reality conversion, I strongly recommend this book as a road map to your ultimate personal destination.

— **Paul Beran,** President/CEO, Advertel, Inc.

Dr. McCorkle has done what every author hopes to do — bring readers back to themselves. This book takes us through the simple yet profoundly effective steps that are necessary to develop the keys to unlock the heart. Her process provides valuable insights almost immediately and offers the opportunity to heal. There is no greater gift.

— **Dr. Jonas E. Marry, DC,** Family First Chiropractic

Do you want to feel happy, loving, fearless? Are you ready to be proactive rather than reactive? Are you willing to love and respect yourself, others, and life circumstances? If so, then Dr. Katie has the ticket. She has managed to put together a very rich set of strategies and tools that help you truly breakthrough past challenges. From personal experience I can guarantee that if you follow her simple yet profound daily reflections, your life will forever be changed for the better, and you will make an even bigger contribution to the world than you ever thought possible. Dr. Katie lays the groundwork to becoming a real world server.

— **Amy Foster,** CEO, Unbridled Performance:
The Center for Team and Leadership Breakthroughs

A Balanced Heart will be a welcome addition to our Women Veteran's Program curriculum. We encourage the women to be proactive in their transformation and healing as we engage in empowerment strategies. Using the 10 principles will help each veteran achieve the goals they have established for their success. Dr. Katie delivers a powerful formula that we embrace.

— **Dr. Lenore Hill, PhD, DPC, BCETS,** Founder and President,
The New Jersey Women and Children Veteran's Supportive Housing program
and author of *It's Not Only Bricks and Mortar: A Comprehensive
Guide to Veteran Transitional Supportive/Safe Haven Housing*

A Balanced Heart takes the reader on a wonderful discovery of happiness. Whether you are wondering why a particular aspect of your life is not working or you're ready to go on a journey of complete self-transformation, this book will help you find the answers. It will challenge you in a positive, encouraging way to grow and change in the happiest of ways.

— **Desiree Butter, MD,** Colonnades Family Practice

For many years I worked hard at improving my relationships with myself and others. Despite participation in many conferences and programs, I was not able to achieve the success I have had with this book's 10 Principles. I have become happier and more optimistic. My relationship with my family has improved so much that we are actually enjoying each other's company for the first time in years. Thank you, Dr. Katie, for "seeing" me and reminding me of who I am.

— **Anna,** Balanced Heart client

A Balanced Heart:

10 Weeks to Breakthrough

DEDICATION

This book is dedicated to all dreams everywhere
as a prayer for their manifestation.
Especially, this book is dedicated to
the big dream for my life . . .

Balanced Heart Healing Center

. . . and to each person who plays a role in its development
and lovingly nurtures its growth.

Thank you . . . with all my heart, thank you!

Proceeds from this book support the Balanced Heart Healing Center.

*Your vision will become clear only when
you look into your own heart.
Who looks outside, dreams;
who looks inside, awakes.*

CARL JUNG

❧

*Your task is not to seek for love,
but merely to seek and find
all the barriers within yourself
that you have built against it.*

RUMI

TABLE OF CONTENTS

ACKNOWLEDGEMENTS

I thank God for my own breakthrough, and for the 10 Principles of unconditional love that empowered it. I cherish every moment of this amazing journey, and every lesson I learned. With blessings of gratitude, I celebrate the many people who helped me with this book along the way, some in ways they don't even know. Most importantly, I thank my clients and friends, who provide the mirrors in which I see myself, and where I still have work to do. You are my most faithful supporters, and inspired me to develop the tools and strategies I now share with others.

I owe a special debt of gratitude to the people who believed in me before I was able to believe in myself. Rev. Roxanne Wilson helped me to see my relationship with God in new ways, and guided me on the path until my eyes were opened. Before I had any idea that I was or could be an author, Burke Allen encouraged me to "write the book!" Dorothy Gold, Ph.D. listened with interest to all my unformed ideas, and validated their worth. Bill Waldron provided encouragement and moral support. David Parker inspired me with tales of how publishing his books transformed his life. AJ Puedan gave me a bigger vision of myself before I had any idea what the dream really was, and Terrell Burdick nudged me by saying that I had a special message to offer. Because of the faith and encouragement you and many others gave me, I persisted.

I am especially grateful to my late father, George McCorkle, who not only loved me unconditionally, but also taught me the power of books to change lives, and modeled in his own life the courage that this journey has required of me.

I am eternally grateful to my beloved cats Fred, Marissa, Cloe, and Zoro, who patiently (and sometimes not so patiently) sacrificed their own needs in service to my work, and whose unconditional love sustained me during the writing of this book. I am grateful to my dear friend, Joan Mann, for bringing all of my cats to me, and nurturing me with her loving friendship.

Thank you also to the people in my life with whom I have found it a challenge to get along in the past, especially my late mother, Harriet T. McCorkle. You taught me to slow down and pay attention to what was working in me, and what really wasn't, so I could make within myself the adjustments necessary to grow a balanced heart. Without you, I would be far less self-aware.

Thank you to the people in my life who have brought me joy and broken my heart, for you taught me how to heal myself, so I can now teach others how to heal themselves too. The lessons I learned from you are reflected in these pages.

There are a great many people, including both current and past members of the Board of Trustees, as well as dedicated students and volunteers, who have contributed to the vision and the reality of Balanced Heart Healing Center's development. Without you, neither Balanced Heart Healing Center nor this book would be possible. I thank each of you with all my heart for your part in our collective gift to the world!

Thank you to all the many people who encouraged me and helped make this book a reality as it neared completion, especially my editor and publishing consultant, Gina Mazza, whose insightful editorial comments shaped this into a far better book than it would have been without her. Thank you also to RJ Thompson, my graphic designer and website developer, who is making this book accessible to the world, and to Holly Rosborough for being so easy to work with and for a beautiful layout.

To all, I cherish the gift of your friendship, and look forward to hearing the stories of your journeys. Please know how very much I love you!

Dr. Katie

October 25, 2010

INTRODUCTION

"Write the book!" my coach exhorted me with increasing urgency. "You have something to say" others echoed. The only problem was that I didn't know what the book was to be. I had never thought of myself as an author or imagined writing a book. Frankly, I didn't know how to begin. So I just started writing a journal…anything that came to my mind…in hope of discovering my book. Six years and many hundreds of pages later, it finally dawned on me that my book was to be a journal.

In my private psychology practice, I often recommend to clients that they keep a success journal, because journaling about your successes has so many benefits. It keeps you focused on your goals and aware of your progress, keeps you mindful of and grateful for all that's going right in your life, balances what seems to be going "wrong", and provides an opportunity to appreciate yourself. Perhaps the most important benefit is that it expands your self-awareness about how you are creating your life. It is a way to love your journey, and breakthrough to the fulfillment of your dreams.

Suddenly, I knew that I could make the process of birthing dreams easier and quicker for others if I simply wrote the book. Then, in a flash of inspiration, the essence of it poured through me in 10 days. That's the way dreams appear…at the exact moment when preparation meets inspiration. We never know when that moment will be, but my experience is that everything in life is preparation for and a preview of either a breakthrough or another learning opportunity yet to come.

Everything begins with a thought. Whether that thought is positive or negative, whether it stretches you towards all you can be or keeps you trapped in fear, each thought creates the joys, opportunities, and sorrows in your future. So take charge of your thoughts, and make sure they serve the conscious creation of your desired future. Pay careful attention to your heart. Allow its goodness to nourish your thoughts and pour out into your life, creating one breakthrough after another. Love is the soil in which all things grow.

This book is a guided success journal offering you the tools and strategies that have helped me to breakthrough, and brought me to this point in fulfilling my dreams. They now help my clients and students to birth their dreams as well. This book will teach you how to step into the flow, and empower you to create your happiest, most fearless, and balanced life.

The good news is that it need not take you anywhere near as long to create your breakthrough as it took me. By the time you complete this journal, you will have experienced using all the tools and strategies you will ever need to reduce stress or manifest any dream. Then it's just a matter of using them more consistently and applying them in a focused way.

Since the first time you do anything is always the most difficult, it only gets easier every time you practice using these tools and strategies. After the first time, the journey is all about becoming more consistent in being who you want to be, and doing what you already know how to do. Practice does indeed make perfect. Going through the journal more than once will help the tools and strategies to become second nature to you.

The reason that living and teaching these 10 Principles is so important to me is because I have discovered in the process that I am so much more than I ever imagined possible. And so are you! The 10 Principles have taught me balance, trust, and non-attachment. They have opened my heart to passion and energy that I never knew before. They opened my eyes to possibilities I never imagined, and showed me the path to birth my own dreams. Now I want to offer that gift to you.

You can choose to use this journal either on your own or with others. Perhaps you want to journal and share experiences with friends, or your book group, or a small group in your faith community. Additional support is available through individual or group coaching by calling toll-free 866-DR-KATIE (866-375-2843). My team and I support people everywhere.

All the answers you've ever wanted or will ever want for the rest of your life already lie within you. This book will help you learn how to use all your relationships, life circumstances, and external events to grow a balanced heart, and become aware of the answer you want at the moment you need it. It also will help you to develop grace and passion as you pursue your dreams.

Manifesting your dream may not be easy, and you are likely to encounter both internal and external "obstacles" along the way. Fear not! These speed bumps help you to slow down and pay attention. They are your teachers, the "faith strengtheners" that help keep your heart balanced so you can continue to grow.

My prayer for you is that as you engage this journey of self-discovery and empowerment, you quickly and easily breakthrough everything that has held you back from living your most balanced, authentic, and passionate life. As you birth your own dreams, you inspire others to birth theirs, so open your heart to who you might become, and discover the love you've always wanted! ❦

WHAT IS A BALANCED HEART?

A balanced heart is one that treats both self and others with love and respect equally. It is open and transparent, bearing no secrets, simultaneously self-aware and engaged with the world, self-supporting, unselfish, and non-judgmental. It envisions many possible outcomes and paths to reach them. People with balanced hearts are proactive, not reactive, and they appear on the outside the same as they truly are on the inside. Their thoughts, words, and deeds consistently express joy, peace and loving kindness, so it is easy for others to know who they are. A balanced heart sees both the positive and negative, and chooses to take in and express only the positive. A balanced heart releases all negativity safely without making either self or others "pay" in some way. From all of life's experiences, a balanced heart learns valuable lessons and grows towards unconditional love. This is a big dream!

Healing your inner and outer world with love is the only strategy that has any chance of success, for love is always the healer. As with any big dream, you must start small, within yourself, and allow your success to grow. Just like babies, that is how dreams are birthed into the world.

It begins with self-healing and learning to love yourself unconditionally, the way God loves you. As you experience success in loving, accepting, and forgiving yourself, you have more love to offer others as well. After all, you can't give anything that you don't already have.

Isn't it miraculous how your love grows when you give it away? I'm not speaking of conditional love, which is the act of loving with the expectation of getting something in return, or loving only when you're getting what you want (and being unloving when you don't). I'm talking about a much purer gift: love that is offered simply for the joy of giving and which seeks nothing in return; love that is received in faith that the intention is good, even when the expression is less than perfect. This is the love of a balanced heart, whose peace is undisturbed whether others are doing what you prefer or not.

Yes, you can learn to love this way, and this journal will assist you on that path. Each success is a small step towards the goal of releasing your attachments with love and joy, so be sure to notice. By focusing on one tool or strategy at a time, you take a baby step each day towards realizing your dream of learning to love yourself, other people, and your dreams unconditionally.

Whatever you focus your attention upon expands in your life. As you focus on what you already know and love about yourself and others, on what you already enjoy doing, on noticing what you and other people are doing "right" in the present moment, on what inner strengths support you through challenging times, and on what opportunities appear just so you can demonstrate your heart of gold in the external world, that love multiplies and you become self-supporting — FREE to give love without strings or agendas, without needing or fearing anything from others.

Throughout your life, you may notice that you return to the same themes again and again. If you have paid attention to what your experiences have taught you, then each time you experience a recurring theme in your life, you do so with deeper self-awareness, compassion and acceptance—in other words, with a more balanced heart. Imagine how it might change your life to focus on your successes over and over again, each time with greater self-love and acceptance.

Sharing your successes and progress towards manifesting your dream has great power to inspire others, especially if they have seen you struggle in the past. As you improve at noticing your own successes, it becomes easier to help your friends, family and co-workers to notice theirs as well.

And of course, in the same way that helping yourself also supports them, so does helping them also support you. Whether it's a lot or a little, you give what you believe that you deserve to receive, and you receive what you are inspired to give.

At the beginning of the journal, you will find two lists: "What Works" and "What Doesn't Work." These pages are blank because you haven't yet identified how you inspire yourself to succeed, grow and expand your comfort zone beyond where it's ever been, as well as how you slow or limit your growth and progress towards birthing your dream. When you know which strategies work best for you (and which ones don't), you are empowered to make conscious choices that enable you to create the life of your dreams. Every time you recognize a strategy for success or challenges, write it on one of these two lists. Strategies on the list of "What Works" are your breakthrough strategies.

The roller coaster of life goes both up and down. It's just as important to know how you may take yourself down, how you slow your growth and create what you don't want in your life. This gives you a real choice to create progress or repeat a lesson. Identifying how you create "life's potholes" allows you to avoid those behaviors and experiences, to steer around them. It gives you a choice to do something different because you can't intentionally change anything outside of your awareness. When you know what isn't working for you, then you can focus your attention on substituting thoughts and behaviors that you know do work, or that you imagine might work. Avoiding what's on your list of "What doesn't Work" reduces your stress, balances your heart, and helps you progress towards your breakthrough. As you do more of what works, and less of what doesn't, you create the life of your dreams. ❧

WHAT WORKS:

(Thoughts, words and actions)

WHAT DOESN'T WORK:

(Thoughts, words and actions)

_____

_____

_____

_____

_____

_____

_____

_____

_____

_____

_____

_____

_____

_____

_____

_____

_____

_____

_____

_____

_____

_____

_____

_____

_____

_____

_____

_____

_____

_____

_____

_____

_____

_____

WHAT WORKS:
(Thoughts, words and actions)

WHAT DOESN'T WORK:
(Thoughts, words and actions)

_____ _____
_____ _____
_____ _____
_____ _____
_____ _____
_____ _____
_____ _____
_____ _____
_____ _____
_____ _____
_____ _____
_____ _____
_____ _____
_____ _____
_____ _____
_____ _____
_____ _____
_____ _____
_____ _____
_____ _____
_____ _____
_____ _____
_____ _____
_____ _____
_____ _____
_____ _____
_____ _____

HOW TO USE THIS JOURNAL

❧

Do you know how or what you wish to breakthrough in the next 10 weeks? If you do, your dream can be your "lab practice" as you travel through this journal. Choose a dream that you are willing to believe you can achieve in the next 10 weeks and that's enough of a stretch that you must invest faith, effort and commitment to accomplish it. It can be a dream all its own, or a piece of a larger dream. It may be a dream of creating or healing something within yourself, or of giving some gift to the world. All dreams are worthy!

When you're stressed or out of balance, you aren't able to commit fully to the dreams that are already in your heart. Balancing your heart releases the stress, so you can commit more deeply to your dream, and thereby to yourself. If you aren't yet sure what your dream is, that's okay. Traveling through this journal and developing a balanced heart will lead you towards discovering it. Just pay attention to what brings you joy, and your joy will lead you to your dreams.

Begin now by writing here whatever you know about the dream to which you wish to breakthrough (warning: it may grow or change as you pursue it).

_____

_____

_____

_____

_____

_____

_____

_____

If you can, describe the essence of your dream in just one sentence, and keep this in the forefront of your mind at all times:

_____

_____

_____

This journal consists of pages upon which to document 10 weeks of your breakthrough to success. Each page has a question, "thought starter" or experience to inspire and focus your writing for the day. You may find it helpful to read each day's inspiration in the morning and journal your reflections in the evening. Take special notice of which exercises you find easy or difficult, and which ones you enjoy or resist. This will point the way to lessons you already have learned, as well as your "growing edges", or where you are out of flow and resisting yourself.

Please don't limit yourself to doing only the exercises in this journal. Feel free to make up your own exercises or "experiments" as well. These exercises are merely a jumping off place to help you get started on your journey of self-discovery, and to make it more fun to keep a journal.

When you're done with the day's topic, feel free to write also about other successes that you've experienced and noticed that day. Each day, be sure to notice and record every step you took, no matter how small, towards realizing your dream.

If you miss a day or drop out for a while, don't give up. Just pick this journal up when you feel ready again and everything you've gained will still be there. Nothing is ever lost! If you feel drawn to focus on the principles out of order, please do. I trust that your inner wisdom knows best where your work is to begin. When you finish, you still will have documented 10 weeks of your successes.

In order to speed your progress towards all of your dreams come true, you may want to complete this journal more than once. If you have received it in electronic format, you are welcome to print it for your personal use as many times as you wish. Please invite your friends and family to purchase their own copy, or support them by purchasing a copy for them. Integrity with U.S. copyright law is good for the soul. ❧

WEEK 1 | OPEN YOUR HEART AND TRUST

Your essence is love, and even in the face of unwanted, difficult, or fear producing circumstances, it is possible for you to act from a place of love deep inside you. The more clearly and deeply you know your loving essence in all its aspects, the easier and faster you grow in confidence to express that love consistently at all times. This is the adventure of life!

If you haven't already, now go to www.balancedheart.org to download and listen to the "Heart of Gold" meditation. This meditation will help you to discover your loving essence and describe it in just a word or two. You may know these words the first time you hear the meditation, or you may become aware of them after listening several times. To help you remember who you really are, please listen to the meditation before you begin the journal, and write your one or two words here: (Hint: these words are always positive: love, respect, peace, joy, giving, etc.)

_____ and _____

Now that you know your one or two words, your life is very simple. Your only job from now until the day you die is to BE those words…all of the time, consistently, no matter what you're doing, who you're with, or what's going on around you. This may sound simple, and it's often not easy. However, as you use the tools and strategies in this book, it will become easier. As you slow down to pay attention and focus upon being those words, they begin to flow out of you naturally.

If you think you've attempted and failed at this in the past, take heart! You have merely focused your attention on the times you've fallen short of your goals, rather than the times you succeeded. Focusing on your "failures" pulls you out of balance, causes you to lose faith in yourself, and keeps you stuck in guilt, pain and fear. When your belief (either consciously or unconsciously) is that you're not capable or that you will never be able to accomplish what you want, that belief becomes a self-fulfilling prophecy. For better and worse, what you believe is true for you! Wouldn't you rather view those "failures" as stepping stones, and focus on how they might help you to succeed?

When you focus your attention equally on the times you've succeeded, even in small ways, it brings balance to your self-perception and frees you to move forward toward your dream. For this reason, identifying and uprooting self-sabotaging beliefs is vitally important. If you're feeling anything less than complete inner peace and joy, know that a negative belief is at work in you. Then ask yourself what that negative belief might be, and how you instead might express more of your loving essence words in that situation at that moment.

Enjoy this adventure, and wonder who you might become in the process. Because the purpose of relationships is to experience the joy of giving and receiving love, as you learn to accept yourself and others with fewer and fewer conditions, you may be amazed at how much your life improves. As you begin to accept and heal what you once disliked or judged in yourself, you open your heart and expand your capacity to offer loving acceptance and forgiveness to others as well. When others do not love you in the way you want to receive love, fill them up with your love instead. That way, love continues to flow and you both are blessed. It's empowering to know that adjusting your own attitude can keep love alive in your relationships.

In all likelihood, you have already done this many times either with or without awareness of what you were doing. Think of the times when you have accepted a sharp word without reciprocating, or done something joyfully when no one else would help. Love is always the healer. As you do the work of personal growth, you become an inspiration to others, and bless yourself by opening your heart to all the love around you. In this way, you become a gift not only to yourself, but also to everyone whose life you touch.

Loving attention is the soil in which all things grow, including children, adults, and both positive and negative thoughts. Without love, everything eventually withers or fails to thrive. An open and willing heart does not fear being broken for it accepts all love sources and knows that a bond of love cannot be broken. As you gratefully accept whatever comes your way – lavishing attention on what you like, and withdrawing your attention from what you don't prefer – you know that you can trust yourself to love and be loved at all times. When you perceive and welcome love from another person, your cup is filled; at other times, you are free to pursue your joy by filling your cup from a different source, or by filling someone else's cup.

For everyone, unconditional love is the most basic need, and without it we die or fail to thrive. Attachments to specific outcomes are the conditions we place on our willingness to love and be happy. Unconditional love for yourself is experiencing and expressing your joy. It is asking fearlessly for the love you want from others, and being willing to receive it from any source, including God within yourself, when it is not forthcoming from your preferred external source. Children have a knack for knowing who truly loves them, and those are the people with whom they want to play and spend time. It is only when you are unable to find a source of love (either within or outside yourself) that you fail to thrive. The exercises in this book will help you to discover an inexhaustible and always available love source within yourself.

Unconditional love for another is being willing to accept gratefully whatever you receive from them (either love or lessons), keeping what you like and letting go of what doesn't serve you. Self-trust is knowing that whatever you choose is best for you—because it brings you either joy or awareness of what does not serve you, so that you can make a new choice in the future, a choice that fuels your growth.

An open heart acts only out of love and respect at all times. It is proactive, not reactive. Whether you give it to yourself or someone else, love is an act of faith in a person's goodness. Respect is your commitment to their well-being. A balanced heart loves and respects both itself and others equally. A balanced heart is both free and faithful. ❧

SUNDAY | *Creating Inner Feelings*

What feeling or experience do you want to now create within yourself? Peace, love, joy, relaxation, kindness? On a scale of 0 to 10 (10 = the most/best, 0 = none), write the number that describes where you are now: ___/10. Now, breathe deeply, all the way down into your abdomen so that only your belly moves in and out (not your chest). Inhale into yourself from everywhere in the universe whatever you want to create more of within yourself (peace, love, joy). Now, hold your breath for a few seconds before slowly exhaling whatever you wish to release (fear, stress, pain, negativity, anger). Holding your breath briefly prevents you from hyperventilating. So does exhaling slowly. Do this for a few minutes. If you are not able to breathe deeply into your belly without your chest moving, just keep practicing until you can.

After a few deep breaths, what is the number that describes where you are now with the feeling you wanted to create? Write it here: ___/10. How did you create that change in such a short time? (Hint: relaxing opens your heart and releases fear.) Write this on your list of "What Works." Now, write about how you feel differently inside. Notice the details of what changed in your body while you were breathing deeply, and how you now know that you are more relaxed and connected with yourself. Whenever you want to change how you feel, this is a way to do it.

_____

_____

_____

_____

_____

_____

_____

_____

_____

_____

_____

_____

_____

_____

_____

_____

_____

_____

MONDAY | *Your Loving Essence*

Write again here the one or two words that describe your loving essence, the truth of who you are, which you wrote after you listened to the "Heart of Gold" meditation. If you have not yet discovered those words through the meditation, think of the happiest time in your life, a time when you felt completely safe and totally loved...or the closest you have come to that. What words describe who you were at that moment?

_____   _____

These words can make your life very simple because living them connects you with goodness, both in others and within yourself. It creates ease and harmony in all of your relationships. How did you express your loving essence today? Write about it here:

_____

_____

_____

_____

_____

_____

_____

_____

_____

_____

_____

_____

_____

_____

_____

_____

_____

_____

_____

TUESDAY | *Follow Your Joy*

Giving yourself permission to follow your deepest JOY in every moment is the quickest way to get everywhere you want to go. Just for today, do only what you can do with joy, and do nothing out of a sense of obligation. If you have responsibilities that do not bring you immediate joy, think about the deeper reason you committed to doing those things, and allow that purpose to fill you with joy in the present moment.

Imagine that you are the human face of God to everyone you see today, spreading love, joy, gratitude, safety and forgiveness to everyone you meet. If you are at work, be aware of ways in which your work activities feed your joy and capacity for supporting yourself and others. As you free yourself of your "burdens," you discover that your commitments express who you are. At the end of the day, write about your experiences, especially how people you know well may have responded differently to you than they usually do. Today I chose joy over obligation or "shoulds" when I:

_____

_____

_____

_____

_____

_____

_____

_____

_____

_____

_____

_____

_____

_____

_____

_____

_____

_____

_____

_____

_____

WEDNESDAY | *Random Acts of Kindness*

Every kindness is a success. Describe a kindness that you did today for someone else or your-self, or both. If you can't identify one, then choose a kindness that you intend to do tomorrow. Write your intention here. Write about your act of kindness or your intention here, and after you've done it, check it off here: ❑ I DID IT!

Now, write about the experience of performing random acts of kindness, and some way that it contributed to achieving your own dream.

_____

_____

_____

_____

_____

_____

_____

_____

_____

_____

_____

_____

_____

_____

_____

_____

_____

_____

_____

_____

_____

_____

_____

_____

_____

THURSDAY | *Fearlessness*

Fear is absolute faith in what you don't want. When you instead PUSH ("Pray Until Something Happens") right through your fear, miracles happen. Then fear becomes the doorway to all your dreams come true. One way in which I took a stand for my dream, myself or something I do want today is:

_____

_____

_____

_____

_____

_____

_____

_____

_____

_____

_____

This is different from what I used to do in that...

_____

_____

_____

_____

_____

_____

_____

_____

_____

_____

_____

FRIDAY | *She Loves Me... She Loves Me Not...*

Love is always free, committed and respectful. Here are some ways to know when a person (including yourself) really loves you:

- They *free* you to be yourself and accept you unconditionally (even if it's not who they are or who they want you to be). They don't attempt to change you.
- They *commit* to support your dreams and love what you love, simply because of your passion for it.
- They are *open* and *transparent* about themselves.

Write your thoughts about some ways in which you know when someone really loves you, and about some people who do. One way to do this is to recall a time when you felt completely safe and totally loved, and notice what you and others did to create that feeling in you. Have you told those people lately how much you appreciate them? If you haven't, it's never too late to do it.

Did you include yourself in the list of people who love you? (Ooops, if you didn't!) Write about a time when you truly loved and appreciated yourself.

_____
_____
_____
_____
_____
_____
_____
_____
_____
_____
_____
_____
_____
_____
_____
_____
_____
_____
_____

SATURDAY | *Forgiveness*

Life is a very long series of moment-to-moment choices about what to hold onto, and what to let go. Forgiveness is letting go. Having self-awareness of who you are inside, and how others perceive you, gives you a real choice about what to hold onto and what to let go, so you always express the best of yourself in the world. Accepting and forgiving what you don't like in yourself is the spiritual work of growing into who you want to be. Are you willing to give up who you've been for who you might become? Who do you want to be? What's the one thing you would change about yourself if you could? Now close your eyes, breathe deeply and send loving energy to the part of yourself that you would like to change until you are able to accept it lovingly. This action flexes your unconditional love muscle.

_____
_____
_____
_____
_____
_____
_____
_____
_____
_____
_____
_____
_____
_____
_____
_____
_____
_____
_____
_____
_____
_____
_____

Week 2 | Give and Receive Without Attachment to Outcome

At all times, you are giving and receiving something. The question is what you choose to give (love or non-love) and what you allow yourself to receive from both yourself and others. Are you drawn to people you admire and in whose presence you feel good about yourself? Imagine that one of your arms is the path through which you receive from the world, and the other arm is the path through which you express yourself. Now imagine that each arm has a positive and a negative channel, and turn off the valve to the negative channel in each arm. This practice frees you to give and receive only love. Do you simply do what's in you to do without expecting anything in return (even gratitude)?

Are you able to distance yourself gracefully from people who don't treat you the way you want to be treated, or do you distance yourself with anger? Are you able to accept "no" for an answer, or do you make others "pay" by blaming them when they don't give you what you want? When the world isn't giving you what you want, do you give it to yourself instead? Do you even realize that you can?

Do you make yourself pay by taking other people's judgments personally? If so…OUCH. That creates or maintains a blind spot in you. Not taking a judgment personally validates how far you've come in your personal growth, while reacting with upset reveals a "growing edge" within yourself.

Attachments are the conditions you place on your love. Releasing your attachment to how things turn out is the path to happiness, and freedom to love yourself and others without conditions. It is a demonstration of your trust that all is well, whether it looks that way or not. ❧

SUNDAY | *Ask and You Will Receive*

Unconditional love for yourself is being willing to ask for what you want and accept gratefully whatever you receive in return. When you want something and don't ask for it, it's a red flag that you feel undeserving of it, or fearful that the other person won't give it to you. What support do you want for manifesting your dream? ASK FOR IT, and write about how you felt doing that.

If you're not sure what your dream is or what support you want, then joyfully support someone else's dream just for the sheer pleasure of doing it. It's an even more powerful experience if you choose to support someone who is not supporting you in the way that you want.

_____

_____

_____

_____

_____

_____

_____

_____

_____

_____

_____

_____

_____

_____

_____

_____

_____

_____

_____

_____

_____

_____

_____

_____

MONDAY | *The Joy of Giving*

It's the love you give that makes you truly happy, for then giving and receiving are the same. When you give love to a person or living creature, you also receive the joy of giving. To expect anything else in addition to that joy is asking to be "paid" twice. When you give something with an expectation that the other person will give you something in return, you're just doing business. Love has no agenda.

Write about a time when you experienced great joy from giving love or an act of service to someone who could not possibly repay you—or someone who could, but you truly didn't care if they ever did. If you've never had this experience, give it to yourself today; volunteer at a soup kitchen or pay the highway toll for the person behind you, for instance, and write about how you felt doing it.

_____

_____

_____

_____

_____

_____

_____

_____

_____

_____

_____

_____

_____

_____

_____

_____

_____

_____

_____

_____

_____

_____

_____

TUESDAY | *Compliments*

Think of how you feel when someone compliments you on an aspect of yourself that you don't like. It may be a physical attribute, a behavior or a personality trait. How do you respond? Do you accept the compliment (in other words, love yourself by allowing yourself to receive it) or do you blow it off in some way (that is, judge yourself as undeserving of it)? If you blow it off, breathe deeply and compliment yourself now. Just now, did you allow the compliment to change your negative view of yourself? It's not too late!

Now, think of how you respond when someone compliments you on an aspect of yourself that you do like. How do you respond then? Do you claim it by agreeing and thanking them? Do you downplay it, or pretend to be modest even though you feel proud? Reflect on what your responses say about you, and what you do and don't allow yourself to receive.

WEDNESDAY | *Nothing to Prove*

Do you test other people's love by forcing them do things (buy gifts, behave the way you want, etc.) to "prove" that they love you? The truth is that no one can ever prove their love for you; either you accept that they love you or you don't. If you make people prove their love, then you don't really believe that they do love you.

As you go through your day, be alert to situations in which it appears that someone is being unloving towards you, and choose to understand their behavior instead as a different way of loving you, or as a request for you to love them. Every request for love is also an opportunity to expand your capacity to love more deeply.

Today, also notice the times when someone behaves lovingly towards you until you ask for something they don't want to give. Are you able to respond lovingly when they become angry or withdraw? Do you attempt to coerce them into giving you what you want? Now write about what happened and what you learned about yourself as a result.

_____

_____

_____

_____

_____

_____

_____

_____

_____

_____

_____

_____

_____

_____

_____

_____

_____

_____

_____

_____

_____

_____

THURSDAY | *Mirrors*

What are the beliefs, behaviors and personality traits that you find most difficult to accept in your significant other, co-worker, child or friend? Now, ponder how you do the same thing, perhaps in a different way. How is the mirror that person holds up to you showing you the hurt place in yourself (which only you can fix)? What healed attitude, thought or behavior does this person give you an opportunity to demonstrate? As you either accept or change annoyances in yourself, it will become much easier to accept them in others. What do you now intend to change?

_____

_____

_____

_____

_____

_____

_____

_____

_____

_____

_____

_____

_____

_____

_____

_____

_____

_____

_____

_____

_____

_____

_____

_____

_____

FRIDAY | *Every Thought is a Prayer*

Our thoughts are how we feed our minds, our hearts, and ultimately, our actions. By your thoughts, you create your life. Are you feeding yourself healthy, loving, uplifting thoughts or "junk thoughts", the ones that drain your spirit and energy? The moment you think "Why aren't you supporting me?" the anguish of loss and separation appear. The moment you seed thoughts of love and acceptance, confidence that you can do what you want whether others support you or not, peace and balance are what you receive.

For better or worse, living by the Golden Rule ("Do unto others as you would have them do unto you") is one way you create the world in which you live. For example, if you give kindness to others, you will always receive kindness as well – either from them, from yourself, or from someone else.

Whatever thoughts you give to yourself are also the ones you give to others. It's not the events in your life that cause you joy or stress, but rather, the meaning you give to those events. Are you supporting yourself and everyone you touch with the abundance of your love? That is how to keep your loved ones close. What thoughts are you keeping, and which ones are you allowing to pass you by? Now journal about the following questions:

Something I want to receive from others is…

I gave that to someone else today by…

I can give that to myself by…

_____

_____

_____

_____

_____

_____

_____

_____

_____

_____

_____

_____

_____

_____

_____

_____

SATURDAY | *Grace*

How do you respond when someone doesn't give you what you want? Do you accept it gracefully? Do you find it a challenge to accept "no" for an answer? When you are told "no", do you attempt to make the person change their mind? If so, this is your ego at work, not your grace or your faith.

Think of a time when you let go easily and moved on. Now write about how you supported yourself to remain unattached to the outcome, and what the results of that action were. Write this strategy on your list of "What Works" on page vii.

_____

_____

_____

_____

_____

_____

_____

_____

_____

_____

_____

_____

_____

_____

_____

_____

_____

_____

_____

_____

_____

_____

_____

WEEK 3 | CREATE SAFETY FOR YOURSELF AND OTHERS

Good things happen when everyone feels safe. Balance and respect create safety. Think about it: don't you feel safe with people who respect your needs as much as their own? Self-respect creates safety inside yourself, and empowers you to make choices that balance all of your relationships.

The rules you choose to live by (your values, habits and routines) define your safety and your fears. How much freedom can you give yourself and still feel safe? When you betray your boundaries, you betray yourself. If you don't know what those boundaries are, you don't know yourself or how to maintain your balance. When that is the case, the experiences that you choose will eventually show you what pulls you out of balance and what restores balance to your life.

By paying attention to what does and doesn't bring happiness to your world, you give yourself opportunities to discover, define and expand your boundaries. As you pay attention to what creates happiness both for yourself and others, it becomes easier to foster peace, harmony and safety in both your inner and outer worlds. ❧

SUNDAY | *Balance*

When a relationship is balanced, both people win. When it's out of balance, one person wins at the other's expense. When you are balanced within yourself, you win even if the relationship ends. Write about how your relationships with yourself and others are in balance or not.

What changes do you want to make to bring them into better balance?

_____

_____

_____

_____

_____

_____

_____

_____

One way to figure this out is to think of someone in your life who has accepted you as you are and regardless of what you've done, even when you knew you weren't being nice. That person was experiencing inner balance even though you weren't. How did you feel with that person?

Did you stop making them "pay" for loving you? Write about how you changed because of that relationship and how you might pass that gift on to others.

A time when I felt completely safe and totally loved was:

_____

_____

_____

_____

_____

_____

_____

_____

Anytime you now want to feel completely safe and totally loved, all you must do is remember this moment in time.

MONDAY | *Guard Your Heart and Theirs*

In the same way that you have a choice about what you do with the contents of your "inbox" and "outbox" at work, you also have a choice about what you take into your heart and express outwardly in the world. Are you allowing only love from others to feed your heart (and letting go of the rest)? Are you expressing only the goodness within you and addressing your negative thoughts on your own, without making others pay for them?

Too often, you may take other people's thoughts and actions into your own heart, even if you disagree with them. Taking things personally in this way creates self-doubt and confusion about who you really are.

What creates balance is: 1) taking into yourself only positive thoughts and expressions from others (including insights that may be painful to acknowledge), without taking anything personally, and 2) withholding your negative reactions until you are balanced inside yourself and able to express your thoughts and feelings positively and respectfully. In other words, take in only love and give out only love. Consider the other's views for whatever value they may have for you, and address any negativity inside yourself, without reacting outwardly. Practice this today, then write about what you learned. If you caught yourself slipping, did you remember to be grateful for the self-awareness you obtained as a result?

_____

_____

_____

_____

_____

_____

_____

_____

_____

_____

_____

_____

_____

_____

_____

_____

_____

_____

_____

TUESDAY | *Ask, Don't Tell*

One way of creating safety in a relationship is by asking clarifying questions, and accepting at face value the answers you receive. Asking questions gives you the information you require in order to respect both others and yourself. Choosing to live in fantasyland or attempting to impose your will over another's objections disrespects you both and creates conflict, or sets you up for disappointment.

Is there anyone who has modeled this "ask, don't tell" way of being for you? Today, when you're tempted to tell someone what to do, or give someone the benefit of your great advice, instead ask him or her a clarifying question. This is a question that invites the person to slow down, consider evidence that is compelling to you, and draw their own conclusion.

For example, you might ask "Do you really believe that?" or "Is that the best you can do?" or "Would you like to know what I think?" Teaching children and teens that the best in them is who they really are, and anything less is "out of character" leads to positive self-esteem and self-correcting behavior. When this habit is well established, asking simply "Is that who you really think you are?" or "Are you showing up in character or out of character?" can be a very effective cue to stop and consider what they're doing. You lead the horse to water (so to speak) and then respect without pressure the horse's choice of whether or not to drink. Of course, choosing not to drink has its own consequences.

Ask some clarifying questions today, then reflect on how the people responded differently than you might have imagined, or exactly as you hoped. What did you learn from this experience?

_____

_____

_____

_____

_____

_____

_____

_____

_____

_____

_____

_____

_____

_____

WEDNESDAY | *Creating Safety and Balance*

When you are in balance, you feel comfortable, free and in "flow." How balanced do you feel right now? (10 = totally balanced, 0 = not at all) _____. Journal about the following thought starters.

I know I am in or out of balance when...

Some aspects of my life that are in balance and working well are...

Some aspects of my life that are stressful and out of balance are...

One small thing I can do to bring my mind, body and spirit into better balance is...

_____

_____

_____

_____

_____

_____

_____

_____

_____

_____

_____

_____

_____

_____

_____

_____

When you are out of balance, conscious deep breathing restores balance as you inhale what you want to create and exhale what you want to release. To breathe deeply, inhale air through your nose all the way down into your belly (only your belly moves in and out, while your chest remains still). Hold it for a few seconds, then exhale very slowly through your slightly opened mouth, taking at least twice as long to exhale as you did to inhale. Now take a few more breaths. Inhale peace, love and joy, and exhale stress, fear, pain and negativity...or anything that no longer serves you, and anything you now wish to release.

Check in with yourself again about how balanced you feel, and write the number here (10 = totally balanced, 0 = not at all) _____. Are you surprised by how much balance you created in just a few minutes?

THURSDAY | *Blessed Differences*

The biggest challenge that any relationship ever faces is, "How different can we be and still treat each other with love and respect?" Embracing bigger differences expands you both. Respecting others requires letting go of your personal agendas (ego). Who are the people in your life who could do almost anything and you'd still love them even if you chose not to be with them, just because it's in you to love them or because you don't know how not to love them? Reflect upon what makes them so easy to love and know that you have that same trait within you.

How do you create enough safety in those relationships to embrace very big differences between you?

When you sense that someone is uncomfortable, ask what would make the person feel safer, then do what is asked. Now write about that experience.

_____

_____

_____

_____

_____

_____

_____

_____

_____

_____

_____

_____

_____

_____

_____

_____

_____

_____

_____

_____

_____

_____

FRIDAY | *Flowing Free*

Love is always free. One way to know that you're balanced within yourself is that you feel happy, loving, and fearless. You're in FLOW. Write about a time when you felt this way and about how you created that experience. Be specific. What were you doing? Were you inwardly focused or focused on people around you? What thoughts were going through your mind? When you understand how you created a sense of fearlessness even once, you can create it any time you want. Be sure to write this strategy on your list of "What Works" on page vii.

When you're out of balance, feeling trapped or stuck, what helps you most to re-balance yourself and get back into the flow? If you prefer to withdraw and nourish yourself when you're feeling out of sorts by, for instance, taking a walk in the woods, write that on your "What Works" list.

If it helps you to talk matters out with someone else or ask for others' support, then write that on your list as a reminder to yourself.

_____

_____

_____

_____

_____

_____

_____

_____

_____

_____

_____

_____

_____

_____

_____

_____

_____

_____

_____

_____

SATURDAY | *Safety Rules*

What are your personal "safety rules"? These are the principles that you follow to keep yourself safe and the things you can always do to help yourself feel better balanced. If you don't yet have a list, create one now. If that's a challenge, think about times when you've felt safe or unsafe in the past, and contemplate what you did to create safety in those situations.

_____

_____

_____

_____

_____

_____

_____

Week 4 | WELCOME EVERYTHING AS A BLESSING, ESPECIALLY WHEN IT DOESN'T LOOK LIKE ONE

When germinated in expanding self-awareness and nurtured by love, every challenge holds seeds of growth. When the world is viewed through loving eyes, apparent misfortune is seen as mere illusion and an opportunity for expanding self-awareness and expressing the best in you. So why not welcome it from the very beginning for the blessing that it truly is? Every challenge is a chance to explore higher and deeper parts of yourself than you might have imagined were there before. The times when things don't seem to be going well are your faith strengtheners. They are crucial openings to believe in the full bloom that you cannot yet see. If approached with gratitude, challenges beckon you to seek and find love all around you.

All blessings are mixed. The beauty of it is that you get to choose whether to give your power to the positive or negative aspect by focusing your attention on either what's going "right" or seemingly going "wrong." Here's the importance of that choice: whatever you choose will increase in your life. Which one do you prefer?

Each of us is also a "mixed blessing". The potential for everything exists in all of us, though some of us express our positive or negative aspects more often. Think of others as your personal self-awareness tool. For better and worse, whatever you see in others is a reflection of what is in you, whether you see it in yourself or not. Because likes attract, if it did not already exist in you, it would not be possible to see it in others. For example, when you enjoy others, it reflects the appreciation you feel for yourself. When you are critical or angry towards others, it is a red flag that you dislike that same aspect in yourself. When you see something that you don't prefer in someone else, it is merely an alert to heal that trait in yourself so that you don't make others "pay". In that way, you support and inspire them as well. Are you willing to forgive, and love all of who you are? ❧

SUNDAY | *Blessings in Disguise*

Positive, joyful experiences can teach you how to create more of what you want in your life. Reflect on a recent experience that you wanted to have. How did you attract it or allow yourself to have that experience? If you think it "just happened" without any action on your part, ask yourself how you stepped into the flow, and aligned yourself with that experience. Now add that strategy to your list of "What Works" on page vii.

Difficult experiences can show you what doesn't work, how you can support yourself through challenging times and transform them. Reflect on a recent experience that you didn't want in your life. How did you attract or allow yourself to have that experience? Write this on your list of "What Doesn't Work." How did you lift yourself out of that situation? Write this on your list of "What Works."

_____

_____

_____

_____

_____

_____

_____

_____

_____

_____

_____

_____

_____

_____

_____

_____

_____

_____

_____

_____

_____

_____

MONDAY | *Mixed Blessings*

As stated previously, we are all "mixed blessings" with both positive and negative aspects. Accepting others just as they are, without wanting to "fix" or change them, and without allowing yourself to absorb any negativity from them, is how you (and they) experience the vastness of the love within you. Think of someone who you love deeply for the whole package they are, including the traits you don't prefer. If there's no one like this in your life, then imagine feeling this way about someone. Now write about your real or imagined experience.

_____

_____

_____

_____

_____

_____

_____

_____

_____

_____

_____

_____

_____

_____

_____

_____

_____

_____

_____

_____

_____

_____

TUESDAY | *Giving the Best of You*

Today, be grateful that your happiness depends only on what you put into the world—not on what you receive from it or what others do (unless you choose to embrace their beliefs or give them your power). What do you want to create in the world today? Focus your attention on giving that gift to everyone you meet. Practice giving the best of you by gracefully accepting "no" for an answer when others do not give you what you want or request.

_____

_____

_____

_____

_____

_____

_____

_____

_____

_____

_____

_____

_____

_____

_____

_____

_____

_____

_____

_____

_____

_____

_____

WEDNESDAY | *Expanding Your Love*

At all times, you are giving and receiving either love or non-love (everything else). The question is what you choose to give to the world, and what you allow yourself to receive from others. Are you allowing yourself to receive only love from others, and are you giving only love to others? When someone treats you in a way you don't like or you receive something unwanted, how do you respond? Do you take criticism or resistance into your heart and react in a negative way? Do you use that information to make adjustments and corrections within yourself? Do you allow the experience to pass without negatively affecting your relationship with the other person or yourself? Think of a relationship conflict that you found a way to heal and forgive. Write about how you inspired yourself to love enough to accept what was once unacceptable.

Add that strategy to your list of "What Works" on page vii.

_____

_____

_____

_____

_____

_____

_____

_____

_____

_____

_____

_____

_____

_____

_____

_____

_____

_____

_____

_____

_____

_____

THURSDAY | *Acceptance*

Love heals and expands! Take a few deep breaths to relax and connect with your inner self. Allow yourself to know an aspect of yourself about which you are often self-critical, and that you are now willing to accept. Don't attempt to think your way through this; just allow that aspect to emerge into your awareness as a gift from your "inner knower." Through the power of your intention, send loving energy to both the knower within you, and the formerly criticized aspect of yourself that you are now willing to accept. Is this the way you have come to accept things in the past, or have you used another process? If so, put both on your list of "What Works" on page vii.

Now wonder about other ways that you might come to accept the "unacceptables" in your life, and contemplate how they may be blessings to you. Be grateful for that lesson and write about it. This lightens the negativity that you've been carrying.

_____

_____

_____

_____

_____

_____

_____

_____

_____

_____

_____

_____

_____

_____

_____

_____

_____

_____

_____

_____

FRIDAY | *Blessings and "Curses"*

Identify what have appeared to be curses in your life, either past or present:

a person _____

a situation _____

a circumstance _____

Now, identify and write about ways in which these same "curses" led to blessings in your life or might lead to blessings now. Examples of blessings might be increased self-awareness, learning an important lesson, the positive transformation of a relationship, or an experience you otherwise would not have had.

_____

_____

_____

_____

_____

_____

_____

_____

_____

_____

_____

_____

_____

_____

_____

_____

_____

_____

_____

_____

_____

_____

_____

_____

SATURDAY | *Clarifiers and Clouds*

Think of something recent that you didn't want to show up in your life. Get creative and imagine how it might be the best thing that possibly could have happened.

Now, think of a time when you got your own way over someone else's objection, and ask yourself how that experience might have clouded your vision of the truth, limited your awareness, or slowed your growth.

Write about the self-awareness that both experiences brought you.

_____

_____

_____

_____

_____

_____

_____

_____

_____

_____

_____

_____

_____

_____

_____

_____

_____

_____

_____

_____

_____

_____

_____

_____

_____

Are you a "glass half full" or "glass half empty" kind of person? There's no right or wrong answer because each of us must find a way to balance ourselves and move through the positive and negative aspects embedded in all experiences. The important thing is to see your glass as both half full and half empty. Then you are free to choose whichever perspective serves you better in that moment.

Guilt feelings make you aware that you are out of integrity with yourself in some way. When you hold onto guilt rather than make a change, however, you keep yourself attached to that negativity, and out of integrity with yourself.

What defines your character is what you do after you become aware of a "mistake." Do you deny it, blame someone else, or obsess over self-criticism? Do you right the wrong? Do you apologize or forgive yourself? Making a change is a commitment to forgiveness, and frees you to move forward. Taking a leap of faith outside your comfort zone in order to make a new choice expresses your faith in goodness. It is an expression of self-love.

When you allow yourself either to succeed or to fail without losing faith, this is forgiveness in action. Then you can see the glass as both half full and half empty at the same time. You know the potential, and see where you fell short. You are aware and appreciative of both how far you've come and also how far you have yet to grow. Focusing on what you've already accomplished increases your self-confidence that you can succeed in the face of future challenges, and gives you power and motivation to realize new dreams. This balanced awareness frees you to see the goodness in where you are now, and be fearless as you take a leap of faith into the future. This balanced awareness keeps you grounded in the present moment, free to grow.

Seeing goodness in yourself fosters self-trust. Then, even if you are unable to see goodness in others, you still can see it in yourself as you respond to them lovingly. Expressing your faith in goodness releases all negativity. It frees you to focus on what is going right, so you can move forward with confidence and faith. ❧

SUNDAY | *Good Relationships*

Think of someone in your life who is good to you and for you every time you're together. How did you create such a happy relationship? Wasn't it by seeing the goodness in them and reflecting it back? How do you behave differently towards this person than you do towards others? Are you more likely to believe that their motivations are positive, to give them the benefit of the doubt? Surely, not every relationship in your life is as good as this one.

In some relationships, differences are enriching and supportive of growth. In others, differences may be challenging if you are attached to specific outcomes. Challenges are only a different way of supporting your growth if they inspire you to let go. When you realize that your attitude towards differences determines the nature of a relationship, you are empowered to create what you really want.

Now imagine being with someone with whom you have a difficult relationship. Imagine that they are doing the best they can, even if you don't like the result. Either in your imagination or in reality, practice accepting the person while balancing yourself inwardly and holding a higher vision for their behavior, and yours. Look for the goodness within them. Find the degree of closeness or distance that you can sustain without reacting negatively.

Now write about this experience, and write on your list of "What Works" the attitudes and behaviors that create the relationships you want with yourself and others.

_____

_____

_____

_____

_____

_____

_____

_____

_____

_____

_____

_____

_____

_____

_____

_____

_____

MONDAY | *Power*

As I've mentioned several times, all blessings are mixed. Both positive and negative aspects are present at all times within ourselves, and we get to choose which ones receive the power of our attention, and which ones we express to others. Today, choose on purpose to focus on the positive aspect of a difficult situation or personal challenge. Ask yourself how it might be a blessing to you. Also notice a time when you chose to focus on the negative aspect or became reactive to someone, and be grateful for the self-awareness it brought you. Only when you are self-aware do you have a real choice about whether or not to change. Be grateful that you have the ability to make a different choice next time, and write about what you learned.

_____

_____

_____

TUESDAY | *Hearts of Gold*

Wherever you are today – at work or the mall or out with friends – go looking for the heart of gold in everyone you encounter. Don't stop until you find it, and be unwilling to entertain negative thoughts about anyone, including yourself. Now write about your experience.

_____

_____

_____

_____

_____

_____

_____

_____

_____

_____

_____

_____

_____

_____

_____

_____

_____

_____

_____

_____

_____

_____

_____

_____

_____

_____

WEDNESDAY | *Gratitude*

Gratitude expresses your awareness of goodness. By focusing on something for which you are grateful, even in situations that appear disastrous, you demonstrate your faith that goodness prevails. At the very least, a difficult situation or person is your "faith strengthener," offering you a powerful experience of your capacity to love and experience goodness within yourself. Write about a person or challenging circumstance for which you now feel grateful.

_____

_____

_____

_____

_____

_____

_____

_____

_____

_____

_____

_____

_____

_____

_____

_____

_____

_____

_____

_____

_____

_____

_____

_____

_____

_____

_____

THURSDAY | *One With Your Creator*

When you love and trust yourself completely, you are one with your creator. There is no neediness or self-doubt to bring darkness into your life. Focus your attention inwardly and breathe deeply until you feel quiet and peaceful inside. Now imagine that you are one with God, and view yourself and your life through God's eyes. Feel the power of God's tender love and forgiveness (without judgment) for any mistakes you believe you have made. Allow yourself to experience God's trust in you, a trust so great that there is no desire to change you in any way… only to free you. Then write about your experience.

_____

_____

_____

_____

_____

_____

_____

_____

_____

_____

_____

_____

_____

_____

_____

_____

_____

_____

_____

_____

_____

_____

_____

_____

_____

FRIDAY | *Stretching Your Comfort Zone*

Think of something that someone did or said today that made you feel uncomfortable, and identify your discomfort. Perhaps the person (it could even be you) invited you to step outside your comfort zone, so you experienced your inner resistance. Perhaps the person set a boundary you didn't like, so you experienced resistance from outside yourself. Whether you experience resistance from inside or outside, it is your opportunity to say "yes" to yourself, and "no" to fear.

The best way to stretch your comfort zone is to take a baby step beyond it (not so big as to scare yourself), take a deep breath to establish safety within, and look around to reassure yourself that everything is still okay outside of you. Then do it again, and again, and again…

Now, go looking for the goodness in that uncomfortable experience and write about it.

_____

_____

_____

_____

_____

_____

_____

_____

_____

_____

_____

_____

_____

_____

_____

_____

_____

_____

_____

_____

_____

_____

_____

SATURDAY | *Character*

When you can view others as being loving towards you all of the time (even when they don't express it well) and yourself as expressing consistently loving intentions towards others, then you know yourself as both giving and receiving only goodness and love. When someone behaves in an unloving way towards you, is your default assumption that they really do love you and just aren't showing it right now, or that they don't love you because of the way they're behaving? Do you see the unloving behavior as out of character (making a mistake) or in character (just who they are)? Does your belief about other people's love for you change, or is it constant? Pay attention today, and write about what you learn.

_____
_____
_____
_____
_____
_____
_____
_____
_____
_____
_____
_____
_____
_____
_____
_____
_____
_____
_____
_____
_____
_____
_____

Week 6 | Dream Big

Ever since you were very young, your dreams have inspired you to step outside of your comfort zone, to attempt things you've never done before, to believe in the infinite possibilities of what love and commitment can create. Whether it was falling down thousands of times before you learned to walk or surprising yourself with instant success, believing in your dreams gives power to the goodness within you. Pursuing your dreams expresses your hope, and brings meaning to your life.

Believing in your dreams requires that you welcome change because everything you want is in a place you've never been. Can you trust in goodness enough to move forward in the face of uncertainty? This is what is required in order to realize your dreams.

Another way of looking at uncertainty is that it's the doorway to all your dreams come true. When you overcome fear and step outside your comfort zone, it strengthens your faith in things unseen and calls into question everything you still believe you cannot accomplish. By moving forward despite your fear of the unknown, you step out in faith and demonstrate the depth of your commitment to yourself, and to what you believe. ❧

SUNDAY | *The Gift of Change*

If you had unlimited time, talent and resources, what would you do with your life every day? Are you doing that now in some small way, pursuing that dream one baby step at a time? Even if you cannot devote as much time as you would like to that dream now, are you devoting to it at least some time each day or week? I hope so! If not, what is stopping you? Are you afraid or unwilling to commit?

All dreams (and growth) require some kind of change. If you somehow magically knew that the change you are considering would bring the fulfillment of all your dreams, would you embrace it with your whole heart? Of course you would! And until you do, you'll never know what's possible. Write about times when embracing change was difficult, and you did it anyway. What inspired you to do that? Write it on your list of "What Works" on page vii. If change is a challenge for you, read Marianne Williamson's book, *The Gift of Change*, to get some new ideas about change.

_____

_____

_____

_____

_____

_____

_____

_____

_____

_____

_____

_____

_____

_____

_____

_____

_____

_____

_____

MONDAY | *Claiming Who You Are*

Every time you proclaim your dreams to others, you bring the dream one step closer to manifestation in the world. Not only do they become more real to you when you speak them out loud, but also other people invest their own loving energy in supporting you and holding you accountable to your dreams.

What is the big dream for your life, the one that you hardly dare to speak because it seems silly or so impossible? Go and tell one or more people about it today. If you're not sure what your big dream is, tell someone about a smaller dream you do know and watch it grow! How did you feel doing that? How did the other person respond?

_____

_____

_____

_____

_____

_____

_____

_____

_____

_____

_____

_____

_____

_____

_____

_____

_____

_____

_____

_____

_____

_____

_____

_____

TUESDAY | *Seeds of Faith*

Write about that same big dream for your life, the one that requires a great act of faith to believe you can actually achieve it. Now break it down into smaller steps and record them here. Be sure to include all the preparation steps, some of which you may have completed already. Does your dream feel more achievable now? If not, continue breaking it down until you reach a point where you say to yourself, "Yes, I know I can do this part." Then go do it! Remember the Chinese proverb: "A journey of 1,000 miles begins with a single step."

Remember dreams that you have already achieved and notice how you supported yourself through those achievements. This will inspire your confidence that you can realize this dream also. After all, the first time you do anything is always the hardest; after that, it gets easier and easier with every success.

_____

_____

_____

WEDNESDAY | *Defining Choices*

By your choices you define who you are in each moment. Although some choices feel more important than others, in truth, every choice moves you either closer towards or farther from who you believe you are and the life you want to lead. Write about some times when you made choices that defined you as more than you previously knew you could be. These were acts of fearlessness and faith. Now, think (don't write) about some times when you have defined yourself as less than you knew you could be. Write about what you would do differently if you had it to do over again, and set your intention to do that next time. This is an act of self-forgiveness that will free you to move forward.

_____

_____

_____

_____

_____

_____

_____

_____

_____

_____

_____

_____

_____

_____

_____

_____

_____

_____

_____

_____

_____

_____

_____

_____

THURSDAY | *Progress*

A very big dream is learning to live in the present moment. So often we focus on events in the past or worry about the future. In truth, the present moment is the only place where you can ever create happiness. As you slow down, pay attention, and gratefully "smell the roses" in every moment, the future takes care of itself and the past becomes unimportant. Just for today, practice living in the present and notice what helps you stay present, as well as what pulls you away from the now. These strategies go on your list of "What Works" and What Doesn't Work" on page vii.

FRIDAY | *Believe*

Some people say that "seeing is believing." Others say that "believing is seeing." Reflect on times when you've only been willing to believe in what you could see, and times when your faith was so strong that you chose to believe no matter what happened. How do you choose when to believe in your dream and when to trust only in what you can see? Which works better for you? Put it on your list of "What Works" on page vii. Where is the balance between these two strategies for decision-making? Write about that here.

_____

_____

_____

_____

_____

_____

_____

_____

_____

_____

_____

_____

_____

_____

_____

_____

_____

_____

_____

_____

_____

_____

_____

_____

SATURDAY | *A Deeper Commitment*

Go to the mirror and affirm to yourself, "Yes, I can! I deserve all of the dreams in my heart, and I'm good enough to realize them!" Say this out loud until you convince the person who is looking back at you in the mirror. When followed by even the smallest action, this is a great way to strengthen your faith in yourself and your commitment to your dreams. Do it once or more daily, as needed.

Just for today, keep an index card with you at all times and make a mark on it every time you use the words "can't" or "need." From paying attention this way, what did you learn about how you have been setting limits on your potential to realize your dreams?

_____

_____

_____

_____

_____

_____

_____

_____

_____

_____

_____

_____

_____

_____

_____

_____

_____

_____

_____

_____

_____

_____

_____

_____

WEEK 7 | TAKE RESPONSIBILITY FOR EVERYTHING (NO EXCEPTIONS)

Who is the creator of your life experience? Are you not the one who makes all the choices? While you may not always like what shows up in your life or the choices available to you, you always have choices. At times, it may be tempting to think that circumstances or other people are in control of your life. If so, it is only because you are attached to certain outcomes, and are willing to be happy only if they occur. Then you are part of a co-created experience, and must balance your own well-being with the well-being of others.

However, even in the most dire circumstances, no one can take away your power to choose how to understand what's happening in and around you. Both for better and for worse, you alone determine what your experiences mean to you, and this understanding reflects your beliefs.

Now you know how you create "miracles" and "disasters" in your life. When you go looking for the miracles, you either find them or create them. And when you expect to find disasters, you are blind to anything else. The good news about the ups and downs of life is that both offer an opportunity to slow down and become aware of how you create them. Then you can take responsibility for new choices that will serve you better in the future, and bring your heart into balance.

SUNDAY | *What's Going Right*

Taking responsibility for yourself means not only changing your shortcomings, but also using your gifts. If you're not growing, stretching yourself and using your gifts to the fullest, are you really living? Are you really becoming all you can be? Journal on the following thoughts:

I was really proud of myself today when I…
Something I did today that I've never done before is…
What I learned from it is…

_____

_____

_____

_____

_____

_____

_____

_____

_____

_____

_____

_____

_____

_____

_____

_____

_____

_____

_____

_____

_____

_____

_____

_____

_____

_____

MONDAY | *Inside Out*

Feelings come from inside of you, not from other people or situations. People and situations simply show you what feelings are already there. Feelings are neither good nor bad, right nor wrong; they just are. Feelings are the data you use to make choices about how to behave.

Today, practice owning your feelings—all of them. Whether it's one you prefer or one you don't like, simply be grateful to your feelings for revealing what's inside of you. If you don't like what you're feeling, are you willing to take action to change it? Remember the breathing exercise you learned earlier? Practice it now; breathe in what you want to feel and exhale the feelings you don't want. This is recycling at its best!

_____

_____

_____

_____

_____

_____

_____

_____

_____

_____

_____

_____

_____

_____

_____

_____

_____

_____

_____

_____

_____

_____

TUESDAY | *Love Source*

Insist on receiving your daily requirement of love. There are always two ways to fill yourself with love: by tapping into another's love source, or by accessing divine love within yourself. If you rely on another person to fill your love tank, you may receive what you want or you may be disappointed. If you tell yourself that this person is the only source from which you're willing to receive love, you give that person the power of life and death over you, and set yourself up to feel like a victim if they don't give you love when and how you want it.

When you experience the magnitude and power of divine love within yourself, which feeds both you and others, then giving and receiving are the same, and you always have love to share. Today, how might you connect with the love source within you, and fill yourself?

_____

_____

_____

_____

_____

_____

_____

_____

_____

_____

_____

_____

_____

_____

_____

_____

_____

_____

_____

_____

_____

_____

_____

WEDNESDAY | *Commitment*

Everything in life boils down to where you choose to stake your faith (we all stake it somewhere) and how committed you are to what you believe. Where do you stake your faith? How committed are you to that belief?

Today, commit to a dream or to making a small change in yourself that you've been putting off. What is that commitment? Write about how it feels to commit to yourself, and what has inspired you to do that. Write this on your list of "What Works" on page vii. How do you persist when it is difficult, and flow when life is easier? One way in which you love yourself is by keeping your commitments to yourself and others. Then you know that you are trustworthy. Congratulations!

If you were inconsistent in keeping your commitments today, focus on feeling good about the times when you either succeeded or allowed yourself to be aware of your inconsistency. Notice what stopped you from being consistent. Then be grateful for that awareness, and now make a choice to commit fully to yourself.

_____

_____

_____

_____

_____

_____

_____

_____

_____

_____

_____

_____

_____

_____

_____

_____

_____

_____

_____

_____

_____

THURSDAY | *My Special Gift*

Taking responsibility for everything includes utilizing your gifts fully. What is the greatest gift that you would like to give the world if you could? Even if you are unable to manifest the whole dream right now, what is it in your heart to share today? Take a small step in that direction and notice how you feel inside as you do. Will you commit to taking some small action towards that dream every day?

_____

_____

_____

_____

_____

_____

_____

_____

_____

_____

_____

_____

_____

_____

_____

_____

_____

_____

_____

_____

_____

_____

_____

FRIDAY | *Integrity*

Some people think that if they persist in feeling guilty then they're taking responsibility and restoring their integrity. Not so! Guilt is useful only as a signal that you're out of integrity with yourself in some way. If you hold onto it, guilt keeps you out of integrity. It hides and distorts what you don't want to see in yourself, and keeps you stuck by preventing you from making corrections in your behavior.

Be aware of something about which you feel guilty. Close your eyes and take a few deep breaths, breathing in forgiveness and releasing all guilt feelings as you exhale. Allow your inner guidance to reveal whatever the guilt has hidden from you. Relax into accepting that as a part of you, so that you can forgive yourself and make a change. Write about this experience, especially any parts that surprise you, and the change you intend to make.

_____

_____

_____

_____

_____

_____

_____

_____

_____

_____

_____

_____

_____

_____

_____

_____

_____

_____

_____

_____

_____

_____

_____

SATURDAY | *Change Happens*

Often we don't notice the small, incremental changes that occur slowly over time; yet if you pay attention to these little changes and how you create them, you can speed things up by appreciating yourself for them. As an example, think about how your life was one year ago. Notice something that has changed in you without you realizing it or even intending it. How did you do that? What did you do to cooperate with your best self or allow yourself to accept that change? If it's a change that you like, write your strategy for inviting that change into your life under "What Works". If you backslid, notice how you allowed that to happen, and write this on your list of "What Doesn't Work."

_____

_____

_____

_____

WEEK 8 | LET GO OF WHAT NO LONGER SERVES YOU

Life is an ongoing series of moment-by-moment decisions about what to hold onto and what to release, what to change or create, and what to accept just as it is. Each one of those choices defines you in some way and expresses who you believe you are in that moment.

Letting go (total acceptance) is the answer to just about everything. It develops your patience, strengthens your capacity to love unconditionally, and prevents you from foreclosing prematurely on what you believe is true (for better or worse). It opens a window so that you can see what you had been missing.

Like butterflies, people and experiences wither when they are held too tightly, when you do not free them to realize their own dreams. Children become submissive when they fear losing a parent's love, and rebellious when they feel too restricted or unsupported. Spouses may lose vigor or stray to fulfill their desire for freedom.

The question is how to balance freedom and security within yourself and your relationships. What is the source of your security, and how much is enough? How much freedom must you have? Only by freeing yourself do you discover who you are, and only by freeing others do you discover if they are really yours. If they are, they return to you, just as toddlers return to their mothers periodically for emotional refueling. If they aren't really yours, why would you want to attach yourself to them?

When you let go, accepting what is and allowing yourself to experience joy expresses your faith that you can create happiness in every circumstance. Conversely, "holding on," or attempting to exert control, expresses a lack of trust in both yourself and the other person. In a relationship, acceptance banishes fear; it is an act of faith that whatever is good and loving will always connect you. ❧

SUNDAY | *Flexibility Training*

Do an experiment with yourself today: choose something that you always do in the same way, and do it differently to see how it feels—just because you can. This stretches your "flexibility muscle" and makes it easier to let go whenever you want.

_____

_____

_____

_____

_____

_____

_____

_____

_____

_____

_____

_____

_____

_____

_____

_____

_____

_____

_____

_____

_____

_____

_____

_____

_____

_____

MONDAY | *New Beginnings*

Every moment is a new beginning, if you allow it to be. Here are two important questions to ask yourself: "Am I holding on to what I want?" and "Am I letting go of what I don't want, or what no longer serves me?" If you are feeling anything other than freedom and joy, perhaps it's time to let go.

Make a list of relationships and circumstances that you're holding onto that make you unhappy, as well as the fear that is stopping you from letting go. It may involve a financial issue, a fear of being unloved or alone, or something else. Now identify what has given you the courage to let go in the past, and ponder how those same strategies might support you now.

_____
_____
_____
_____
_____
_____
_____
_____
_____
_____
_____
_____
_____
_____
_____
_____
_____
_____
_____
_____
_____
_____
_____
_____
_____

TUESDAY | *Love with Abandon*

Most people give love in the way that they want to receive it or believe they deserve it. However, loving with abandon means matching the way that others love you even if it challenges your sense of inner balance. We have all been disappointed by someone who didn't love us back in the way that we loved them. It may have been a family member, friend, teacher, employer or other acquaintance. Are you willing to commit to the other's well-being, and to doing things their way, even if it doesn't include the relationship you want to have with them?

"Falling in love" is one of the most powerful attachments we can experience as human beings. It holds great potential to help us find and keep our own inner balance. Are you able to commit more deeply when you want to run away? Are you able to take a step back when the relationship is out of balance or do you continue pursuing it, hoping you can change the other person? What does it take to inspire you to let go and accept what is? Are you able to let go with love, or do you require anger to motivate you to break your attachment to a particular outcome?

Reflect on these questions, then add the answers to your list of "What Works" and "What Doesn't Work" on page vii.

_____

_____

_____

_____

_____

_____

_____

_____

_____

_____

_____

_____

_____

_____

_____

_____

_____

WEDNESDAY | *Paradox*

Attaching to specific outcomes clouds the path to your dreams. It prevents you from seeing that what you want might not be best for you, and that what you don't prefer could be an answer to prayer. Acknowledging your feelings and remaining open to how things might turn out differently often leads to better outcomes than you might have imagined. It releases control and opens the way for your inner guidance to inspire you. Think of a time when you let go of control and received more than you could have imagined. Write about this experience here so you remember that this possibility exists within you. This supports your confidence to let go both now and in the future, and helps you to grow.

_____

_____

_____

_____

_____

_____

_____

_____

_____

_____

_____

_____

_____

_____

_____

_____

_____

_____

_____

_____

_____

_____

_____

THURSDAY | *Freedom*

Attachment to your fears and desires pulls you towards seeing what you already believe, while non-attachment frees you to believe what is real and see more possibilities in a person or situation. Can you let go of your attachment to being right in order to support yourself to be happy with what is? When you are open to both what you previously thought and what you didn't imagine, you free yourself to follow your joy and to see the contents of others' hearts. How is this playing out in your life?

_____

_____

_____

_____

_____

_____

_____

_____

_____

_____

_____

_____

_____

_____

_____

_____

_____

_____

_____

_____

_____

_____

_____

FRIDAY | *Inner Peace*

Inner peace is the willingness to be happy even when you don't like what's happening around you or the way things are changing. It is a willingness to change yourself even when you really like the way things are now. What inner or outer changes would you have to embrace in order to have such peace?

_____

_____

_____

_____

_____

_____

_____

_____

_____

_____

_____

_____

_____

_____

_____

_____

_____

_____

_____

_____

_____

_____

_____

_____

_____

_____

_____

SATURDAY | *Invitations*

When others love you the way you want them to, it feels great; when they don't, it's an invitation to unconditional love for both yourself and the other person. When you can accept love from either source (yourself or someone else) and be happy either way, then you never have to go without the love you want. Today, practice loving yourself and choosing happiness when others do not give you what you want.

_____

_____

_____

_____

_____

_____

_____

_____

_____

_____

_____

_____

_____

_____

_____

_____

_____

_____

_____

_____

_____

_____

_____

_____

_____

Judgments separate the world into good and bad, right and wrong. They deny the reality that the way you treat yourself is also how you treat others, and the way you treat others is also how you treat yourself. Whenever you divide the world, you deny the wholeness of who you are. Judgments separate you from yourself, from your connection to others, and from love. No one wants to be judged, and the judgments you level against yourself (with or without awareness) hurt the most.

Do you make others wrong so you can be right, or take in others' critical opinions as right so you make yourself wrong? Do you keep yourself stuck in guilt and pain by criticizing yourself mercilessly for every mistake, or by agreeing with others who don't see the goodness in you? Remember: we are all mixed blessings and you have the power to choose what to take in to your heart, what to express, and what to release.

Like a seesaw, when you judge someone as better or more capable than yourself, you simultaneously diminish your belief in yourself. When you cast a negative judgment on yourself or another, you set a limit on what is possible. Both of these practices blind you to what may be true, and slow your progress towards manifesting your dreams.

Without loving eyes, only partial truth is visible. When you view yourself with an accepting heart rather than a judging heart, you expand the possibilities within yourself and bless others. As you open your eyes to love, you pave the way for harmony both inside and out. ❧

SUNDAY | *Unstuck*

There is no such thing as a good, bad, right or wrong feeling, only feelings you prefer and ones you don't. As stated earlier, feelings are simply data, a vehicle for communicating information to yourself so that you can make the best decisions about how to behave. When you judge your feelings, you judge yourself and this keeps you stuck in guilt, pain and fear.

Today, instead of judging yourself (or anyone else) for feeling angry, self-critical, weak or otherwise, do this: Close your eyes and take a deep breath to connect with your loving essence within. Be GRATEFUL for the awareness of your negativity, so that you have a real choice about letting it go. Wonder what lie or illusion that negative feeling is exposing, and release all judgment on your exhale. Write here what you learn about yourself from this exercise.

_____

_____

_____

_____

_____

_____

_____

_____

_____

_____

_____

_____

_____

_____

_____

_____

_____

_____

_____

_____

_____

_____

_____

_____

MONDAY | *Play*

Today, do something creative just for the fun of it, and love what you produce simply because it is an expression of you. Allow yourself to be surprised by what you produce, and curious about what you might learn about yourself. DO NOT JUDGE your creative product as good, bad, right or wrong. In fact, don't evaluate it at all. Just love and appreciate it and enjoy the experience of creating it. This is good practice for loving yourself and staying open at other times, too.

_____

_____

_____

_____

_____

_____

_____

_____

_____

_____

_____

_____

_____

_____

_____

_____

_____

_____

_____

_____

_____

_____

_____

TUESDAY | *Curiosity*

There's always more to know than what we're able to see. If you imagine your life as a immense jigsaw puzzle with an infinite number of pieces, how many pieces do you think you are able to see at any one time? Perhaps you see just a few pieces in one little corner. Might the picture you see look different if more of the puzzle were visible? Of course it would, and that's always true. There's always more to see!

Cultivating an attitude of curiosity is one of the best ways to let go of judgments and create a space for the not yet visible to emerge. Relax into a realm of expanded possibilities. Every time you catch yourself making a judgment (negative or positive) today, simply wonder what else is there that you're not yet seeing. Write here what you discover.

_____

_____

_____

_____

_____

_____

_____

_____

_____

_____

_____

_____

_____

_____

_____

_____

_____

_____

_____

_____

_____

_____

WEDNESDAY | *Flow*

Feelings are like a water faucet; they're either on or off. You can't turn on some feelings while turning others off. If you shut down for fear of having feelings that you don't like (anger, fear, loneliness, or others), you close your heart down and limit your experience of love as well.

When your feelings are flowing freely and there is no resistance to them, you are fully alive and aware, living life to the fullest, and knowing that you can choose whether or not to act on any feeling.

When you judge any of your feelings as good or bad, right or wrong, you block or distort your awareness of all your feelings. Just for today, give yourself permission to be aware of all of your feelings without judging them. This is a commitment to being and knowing yourself.

Write about what you learn.

THURSDAY | *Forgiveness in Action*

Often change happens in such small increments that we don't even notice it's occurring. That's why, paradoxically, slowing down and paying attention is the fastest way to reach your goal. It gives you an opportunity to notice your progress, appreciate successes you might have missed, and build your confidence. Today, slow down and notice a way in which you've changed from six months or a year ago, either in your outward behavior or your self-acceptance.

Write about how today you flowed more peacefully through an experience that would have been stressful in the past. Write about something you did today that you would have beaten yourself up for in the past, and how it was different this time. Notice how you felt more accepting today in a familiar situation. All are evidence of greater self-acceptance, or forgiveness in action.

_____

_____

_____

_____

_____

_____

_____

_____

_____

_____

_____

_____

_____

_____

_____

_____

_____

_____

_____

_____

_____

_____

_____

FRIDAY | *Reflecting*

Think of a judgment that someone made about you today, either positive or negative. Now ask yourself: "Do I agree or disagree with this judgment?" The good news is that because it's your life, your opinion counts most. Be thankful for the opportunity to choose whether to hold onto the judgment or let it go. Also remember to be grateful to the judging person for reflecting what they saw and helping you to become more self-aware!

_____

_____

_____

_____

_____

_____

_____

_____

_____

_____

_____

_____

_____

_____

_____

_____

_____

_____

_____

_____

_____

_____

_____

_____

_____

_____

SATURDAY | *Opening*

Succeed in letting go of judgments by doing an experiment with yourself. This exercise demonstrates your willingness to let go of self-judgment and fear. Open up to someone you perceive as a "safe" person and share something you've been holding back. Before you do, make a decision that however the other person responds is okay and decide not to take their response personally. Simply be curious to see how they respond and how you feel while sharing with them. If they respond in the way that you had hoped, great! If they don't, it's an opportunity to love yourself for taking the risk and being willing to support your own growth.

_____

_____

_____

_____

_____

_____

_____

_____

_____

_____

_____

_____

_____

_____

_____

_____

_____

_____

_____

_____

_____

_____

Week 10 | Be the Miracle You Want to Create

What is the miracle you want to create? Do you want to be free, loving, faithful, confident, abundant beyond measure? Whatever you dream of being is indeed possible if only you are willing to believe it and commit your whole heart to it. Half-hearted commitments will never get you where you want to go.

The fastest way to become your own miracle is to notice the first signs of your miracle's emergence in your life right now, even if they are small or inconsistent. This is your opportunity to be the spouse, friend, employee, parent or child you always wanted to be. Lavishing loving attention on all of the small ways that you now demonstrate that miracle is like providing water, sunlight, fertilizer and protective mulch to a garden. It grows!

Look back over your list of "What Works" on page vii and wrap your heart around all of the ways that you now know to create miracles. Thinking those thoughts, speaking those words and taking those actions ever more consistently is how you create the life of your dreams. The power of your intention and focus create greater consistency. Eliminating from your life the thoughts, words, and actions on your list of "What Doesn't Work" also creates miracles.

There may be times on this journey when it is tempting to believe that you are traveling alone, and that is never true. Notice how your inner guidance has been with you and led you over these past nine weeks. Within yourself, you are always safe and held in a sea of love, if you allow it.

Whether love comes from within or outside, flows to you or from you, it is always present. And I am with you in spirit, praying for your success in always being aware of that ever-present love. ❧

SUNDAY | *Consistency*

How consistently honest and positive are your words, thoughts and deeds? The journey to the loving essence within yourself is to become increasingly consistent in expressing the best of you and releasing the worst (safely, of course). Today, pay attention to how consistently or inconsistently positive you are in both your inward and outward expressions. Write about your experience of paying attention and what you learn about yourself today. Allow yourself to know the number between 0 and 10 that describes your consistency (10 = totally consistent), and write it here: _____. How consistent were you before you started this journal? Write that number here: _____. You see… you've already begun to create your own miracle! How did you do it? Write that on your list of "What Works" on page vii.

_____

_____

_____

_____

_____

_____

_____

_____

_____

_____

_____

_____

_____

_____

_____

_____

_____

_____

_____

_____

_____

_____

MONDAY | *Joyful*

The fastest way to be your own miracle is to follow your deepest joy. The tricky part is knowing what your deepest joy really is in any given moment. Sometimes it involves being patient, and sometimes it means doing things you don't especially enjoy. For example, allowing a relationship to evolve slowly rather than forcing or rushing into it may result in a deeper, richer experience (with less risk). Cleaning house or doing yard work may not be your favorite activities, but if you like living in a clean house and taking pride in your home, there comes a time every now and then when those chores are your deepest joy, when doing them frees you and lightens your spirit.

Today, live every moment in the highest expression of the values that you hold dear, and do nothing out of a sense of obligation to others, only out of commitment to who you are. If there are things you must do, first identify the values that make you want to do them. That is how you change "have to's" into "want to's" (which are always more fun). Write about your values and experiences of joy in expressing them today.

_____

_____

_____

_____

_____

_____

_____

_____

_____

_____

_____

_____

_____

_____

_____

_____

_____

_____

_____

_____

TUESDAY | *Loving*

There are many ways in which people ask to be loved. Some give what they want to receive and some act helpless. Others become demanding or angry or test you. Some people ask for what they want using words and others ask through actions or non-verbal behavior. Today, imagine that everyone you encounter is requesting love in some way and notice all of the different ways that people ask for love. Be their love source and offer love freely to everyone who requests it. Then write about what you discover.

_____
_____
_____
_____
_____
_____
_____
_____
_____
_____
_____
_____
_____
_____
_____
_____
_____
_____
_____
_____
_____
_____
_____
_____

WEDNESDAY | *Creation*

If you can dream it, you can be it. Get quiet and relaxed inside, then visualize the future you want to create. Bring it into the present by imagining yourself being that person and living that life now, and write how you feel doing so. If the things that you chastise yourself for or feel undeserving of pop into your mind, just thank them for the self-awareness they bring you, and lovingly release them on your exhale. Then bring your attention back to what you want to create right now, and continue writing about it.

_____

_____

_____

_____

_____

_____

_____

_____

_____

_____

_____

_____

_____

_____

_____

_____

_____

_____

_____

_____

_____

_____

_____

_____

_____

THURSDAY | *Lifting Up*

Write some positive thoughts that are always true for you and that hold the power to lift you out of negativity. It could be thoughts like, "I lovingly release everything that holds me back from my greatest joy" or, "What is the blessing in all of this?" or, "How can I bring more love or peace into this situation?" or something else. You get the idea. Brainstorm some uplifting thoughts and ask your inner guidance to reveal the thoughts that are most powerful for you. Then write them here.

Asking yourself questions is a wonderful exercise because it moves you beyond judgment, sets your creativity in motion, and focuses your attention inwardly. Now copy the thoughts that you like best to keep with you at all times, just in case you want to lift yourself up. Write about your experience of lifting yourself up with these thoughts.

_____
_____
_____
_____
_____
_____
_____
_____
_____
_____
_____
_____
_____
_____
_____
_____
_____
_____
_____

FRIDAY | *Expanding*

In each of us there is a seed of divinity, and as you become aware of and appreciate it, you nurture its growth. Get quiet and relaxed. Connect with your own "heart of gold" and visualize that divine seed growing and expanding to fill your entire body. Imagine your growing "heart of gold" oozing through the pores of your skin into the outer world as it merges with all that is, creating a world where all is one in love. Now write about your experience.

_____

_____

_____

_____

_____

_____

_____

_____

_____

_____

_____

_____

_____

_____

_____

_____

_____

_____

_____

_____

_____

_____

SATURDAY | *Eyes of Love*

As you begin this day, connect with that "heart of gold" within you and return your attention to the outer world with your eyes of love wide open. Each time you encounter someone today, visualize their "heart of gold" within, and see it as the truth of who they are at their essence. Choose to see everything else about them as an illusion. Then write about the experience.

_____

_____

_____

_____

_____

_____

_____

_____

_____

_____

_____

_____

_____

_____

_____

_____

_____

_____

_____

_____

_____

_____

_____

_____

_____

EPILOGUE

Congratulations! You have completed 10 weeks to your breakthrough. Of course, you always can expand beyond where you are, and your biggest dreams may take a lifetime to manifest. The tools and strategies you now know to use will guide you on that path. Return to the beginning of the book, and read what you wrote about the dream you wanted to birth during this time. Where were your breakthroughs?

Write about them here. Whether you came farther than you had hoped or not as far, celebrate your successes! You are the miracle.

_____

_____

_____

_____

_____

_____

_____

_____

_____

_____

_____

At every moment in time, there are two perspectives available. At the beginning of this project, you focused on how far you had to go to breakthrough. Now, you can focus on how far you've come. Both perspectives are equally valid. Focusing on how far you've come brings satisfaction and feeds your confidence and hope for the future, while focusing on how far you have yet to go inspires you to action as you step outside of your comfort zone. Balancing these two perspectives creates happiness in the now. We live in a "both/and" world, not an "either/or" world. Can you now hold both perspectives in your awareness simultaneously? This balances your heart, and keeps you focused on the present moment, the only place where you can create happiness.

As a balanced heart recognizes and appreciates without judgment both how far you've come and how far you have yet to grow, it nurtures future growth by confidently and lovingly embracing the journey in each moment. A balanced heart flows gracefully past speed bumps and detours. Every "now" becomes the fulfillment of a past dream and the seed of a dream yet to be birthed. Here, in the present moment, lies peace, and love, and joy! ∾

ABOUT BALANCED HEART™ HEALING CENTER

In partnership with donors, providers, and clients, Balanced Heart Healing Center is a flourishing community of people learning to live unconditional love for themselves, all living beings, and the planet we share. Believing that all people have something to give and something to receive, it is a holistic health center where people can find unconditional care for mind, body, and spirit, and education to make lifestyle choices for optimal health and well-being regardless of their current health status.

What unites the Balanced Heart community is a passion for integrating the spiritual and the secular in everyday life, and respectfully embracing diverse spiritual beliefs. Balanced Heart Healing Center integrates both traditional and complementary/alternative healing modalities, and supports people to birth their dreams and become all they can be in mind, body, and spirit. The community is founded upon 10 Principles for creating great relationships with ourselves, other people, animals, and the earth itself. These principles guide both the way that we care for each other, and the way Balanced Heart Healing Center does business.

1. Open your heart and trust
2. Give and receive without attachment to the outcome
3. Create safety for yourself and others
4. Welcome everything as a blessing, especially when it doesn't look like one
5. See only goodness (Love)
6. Dream BIG!
7. Take responsibility for everything… no exceptions
8. Let go of what no longer serves you
9. Have no judgments, so truth can be revealed
10. Be the miracle you want to create

Using as our starting point the capacity of the mind to create both health and illness, Balanced Heart Healing Center addresses mental, emotional, and behavioral issues as primary causes of physical symptoms. Incorporated in 2006 as a nonprofit social enterprise, Balanced Heart Healing Center emphasizes integrative wellness care, prevention, health education, and personal responsibility. It offers spiritually-centered cognitive-behavioral treatment and health coaching in collaboration with preventive medicine providers, and evidence-based complementary/alternative practitioners. We expect this approach to lower overall healthcare costs by addressing stress and mental health concerns proactively, before they negatively affect physical health. Serving insured and uninsured clients equally, regardless of financial resources, Balanced Heart Healing Center solves healthcare access and affordability issues by accepting donations for services not covered by insurance and that clients otherwise could not afford.

As a public/private, for-profit/nonprofit partnership leveraging donated services and earned income ventures, Balanced Heart Healing Center demonstrates a holistic model for sustainable community building. It is supported by founder and psychologist Dr. Katie McCorkle, Ph.D., a board of trustees, college and university students, clients, volunteers, and a growing group of integrative healthcare practitioners utilizing a unique and mutually sustainable business model. Please visit us at www.balancedheart.org for more information.

There are several ways to support our work of helping all people to breakthrough:

- Share your services freely with people in your area by becoming a member of the Balanced Heart network as a Healing-Donor or Healing-Partner.
- Tell us your story of healing yourself and/or birthing your dream, so it may inspire others. Email Dr. Katie at drkatie@balancedheart.org to share your story.
- Introduce us to companies and individuals who may want to partner with us and/or benefit from our services.
- Make a tax-deductible donation online at www.balancedheart.org, or mail a check to: Balanced Heart Healing Center, PO Box 730, Warrendale, PA 15095. We are a 501(c)(3) nonprofit organization, and acknowledge all donations for tax purposes.

Blessings of love and gratitude!

Dr. Katie

ABOUT THE AUTHOR

An innovator educated at Stanford University, the University of Pittsburgh, and Harvard Medical School, Dr. Katie McCorkle is a psychologist with decades of experience helping individuals, families, and groups. She is a member of the greater Pittsburgh Psychological Association (past Chair of the Continuing Education Committee), Pennsylvania Psychological Association, American Psychological Association, the Association for Comprehensive Energy Psychology and the National Association of Christian Social Workers.

Dr. Katie McCorkle, Ph.D.

Professionally, Dr. Katie has developed several programs to serve others in innovative ways. She developed an award-winning program for drivers under the influence of alcohol or drugs, was part of the team which developed the first program for adolescent sex offenders in Pennsylvania, and developed an award-winning, multi-agency project to help learning-disabled delinquents develop the academic skills they need to succeed. That program opened the way for implementation of PL 94-142 (special education) in state institutions across Pennsylvania.

Believing that with sufficient organizational and technological resources to match open-hearted healers and people with unmet needs all people could have access to healthcare resources, Dr. Katie founded Balanced Heart™ Healing Center. In partnership with donors, providers, and clients, Balanced Heart Healing Center's mission is to create, fund and launch an integrative health center which offers care for mind, body, and spirit unconditionally, and educates people to make lifestyle choices for optimal health and well-being. Your purchase of this book supports that mission.

In her faith communities, Dr. Katie is a teacher and minister, and has served on national and local boards and committees. Balanced Heart Coaching, the spiritually-centered coaching program Dr. Katie developed, is a system of tools and strategies for living life in greater consistency with your own spiritual beliefs.

For any of the services below, or for bulk book orders for your group or organization, contact Dr. Katie at:

> **Email:**   drkatie@balancedheart.org
> **Phone toll-free:**   866-DR-KATIE (866-375-2843)
> or 724-776-5534 in the Pittsburgh, PA area

- FREE article "Keep Your Love Alive"
- Information about Balanced Heart coaching and coach training to live unconditional love
- Invite Dr. Katie to speak at your organization or conference
- Customized training and consulting for businesses and work groups

www.ingramcontent.com/pod-product-compliance
Lightning Source LLC
Chambersburg PA
CBHW062049090426
42740CB00016B/3073